Flying Fiddle Duets

for violin and cello

Book One   Myanna Harvey

CHP358

www.charveypublications.com

Cover painting by Gregory El Harvey
For more information, visit www.gregharveygallery.com

Flying Fiddle Duets for Violin and Cello

Traditional Tunes, arranged by Myanna Harvey

Table of Contents

Flying Fiddle Duets for Violin and Cello, Book One

John Ryan's Polka

Trad., arr. Myanna Harvey

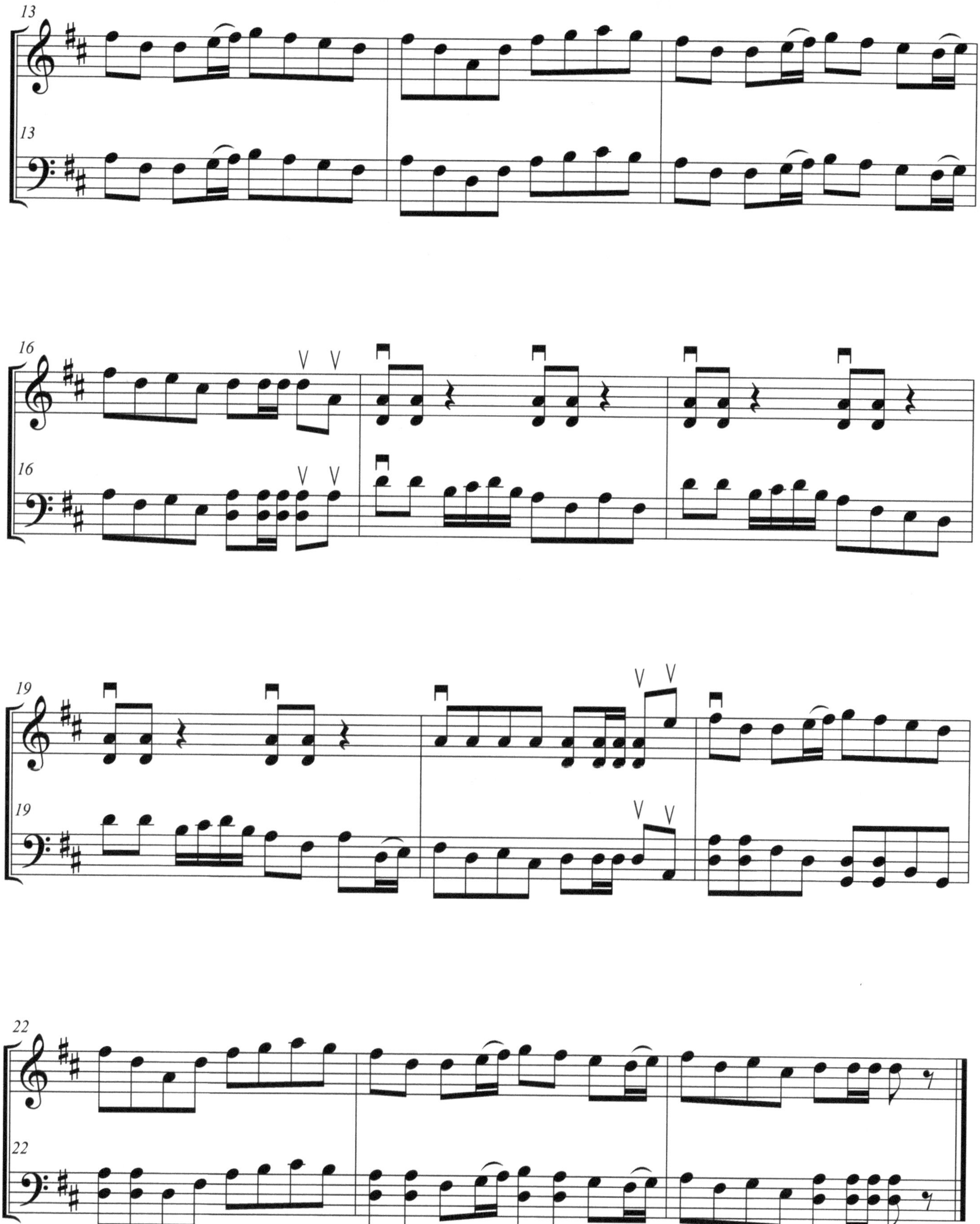
13
13
16
16
19
19
22
22

The Irish Washerwoman

Trad., arr. M. Harvey

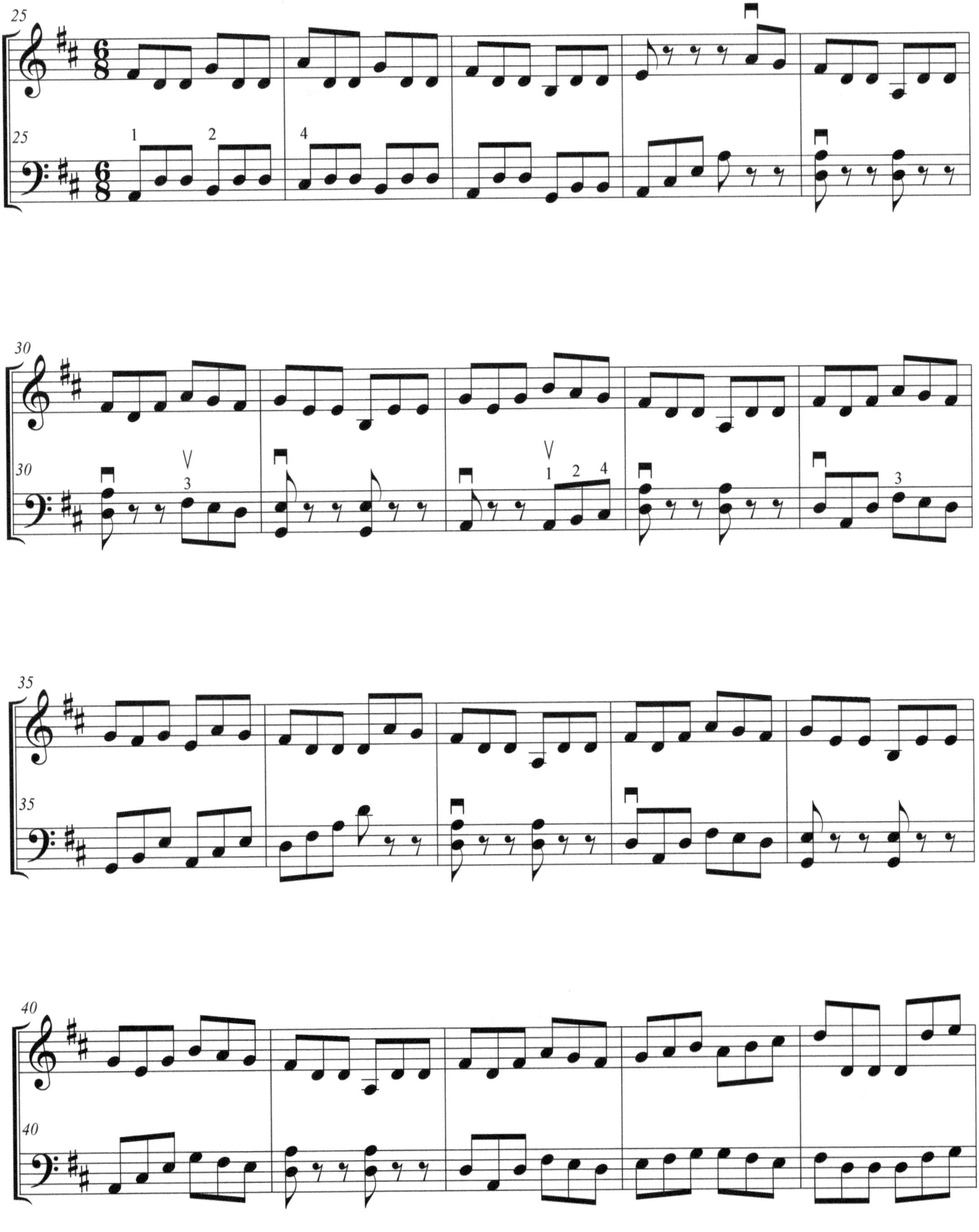

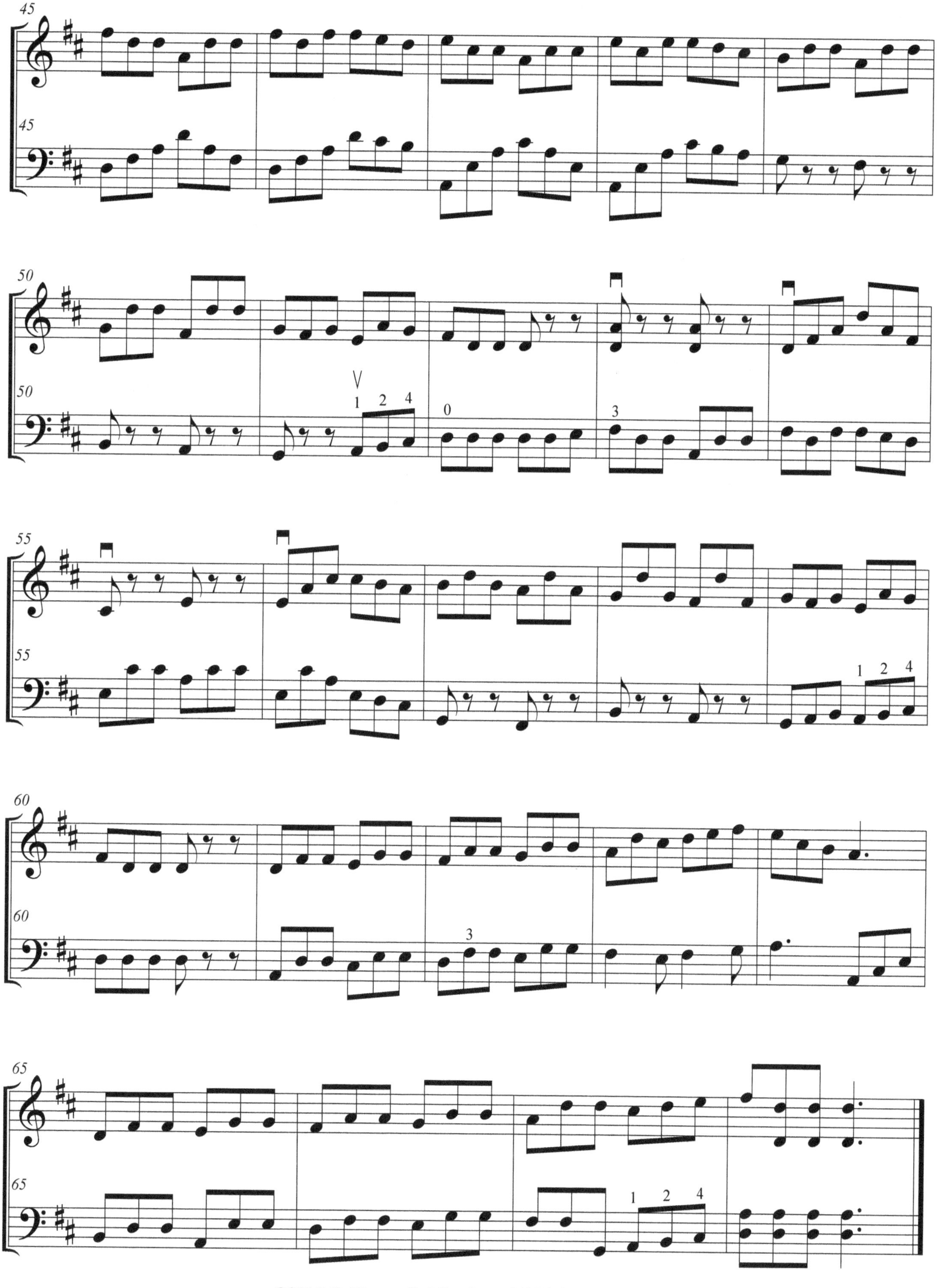

Swallowtail Jig

Trad., arr. M. Harvey

Johnny's Gone for a Soldier

Trad., arr. M. Harvey

Drunken Sailor

Trad., arr. M. Harvey

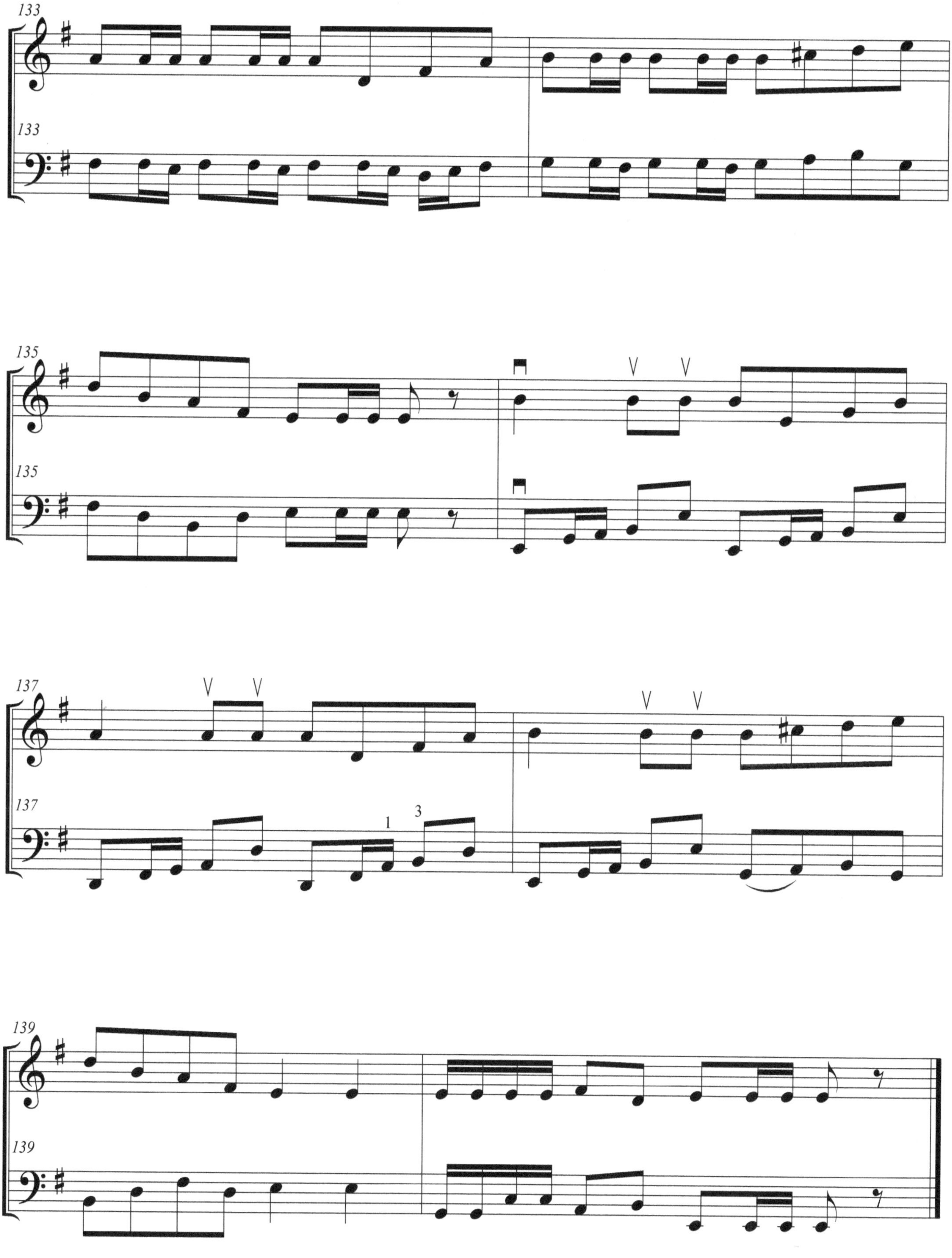
133
133
135
135
137
137
1
3
139
139

Greensleeves

Trad., arr. M. Harvey

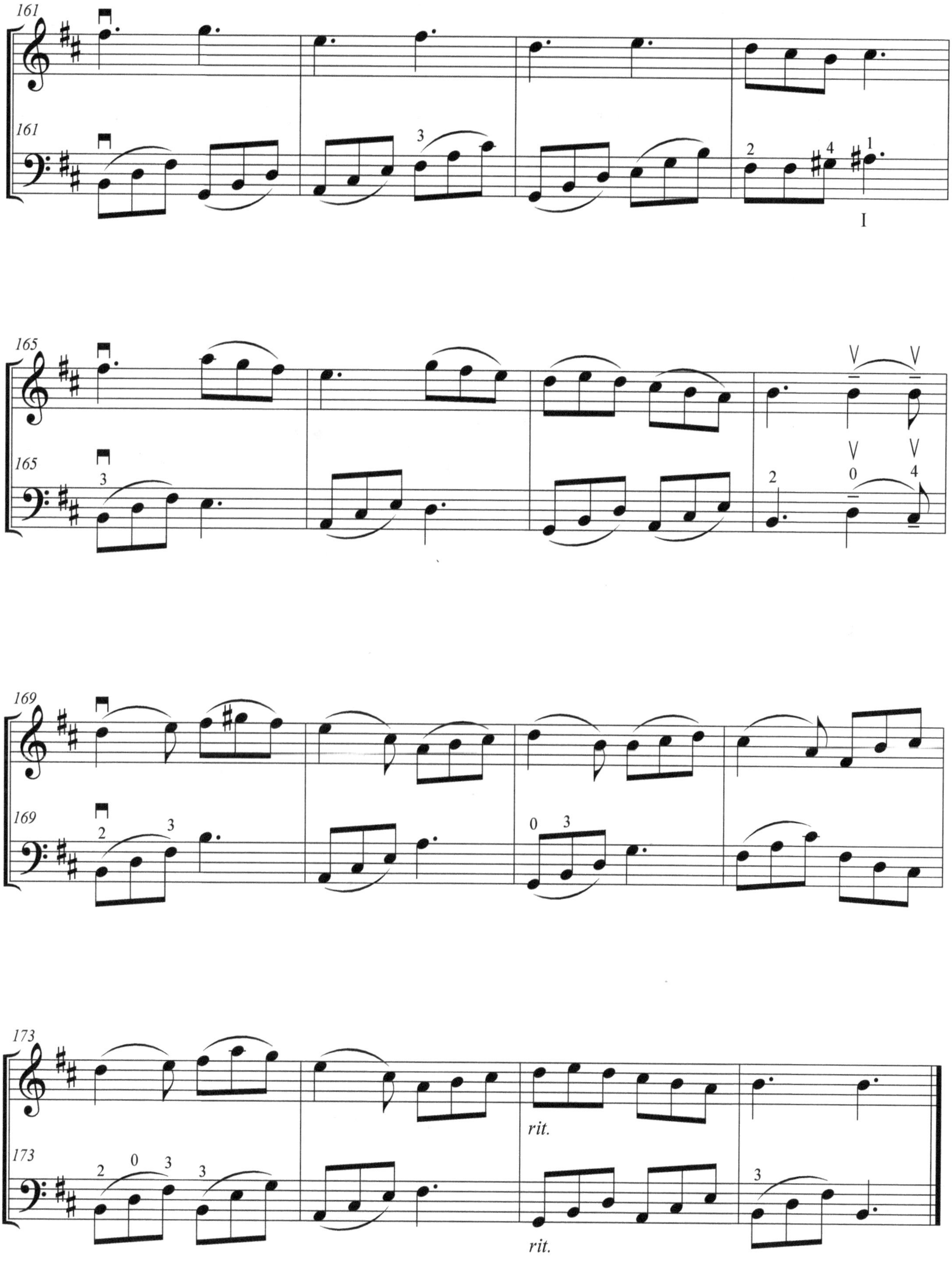
161
161
165
165
169
169
173
173
rit.
rit.

Soldier's Joy

Trad., arr. M. Harvey

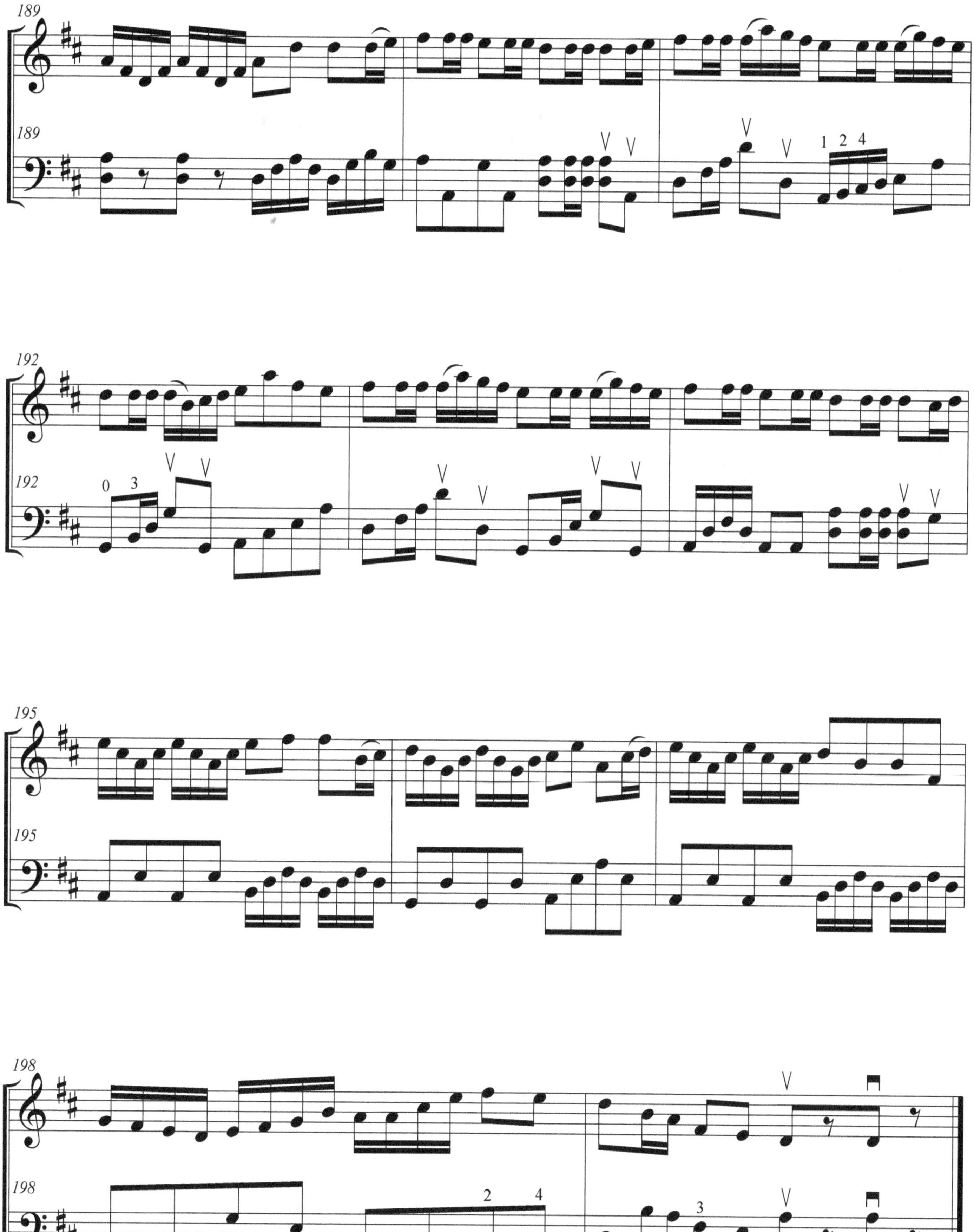
189
189
1 2 4
192
192
0 3
195
195
198
198
2 4
3

Star of the County Down

Trad., arr. M. Harvey

The Water is Wide

Trad., arr. M. Harvey

Lannigan's Ball

Trad., arr. M. Harvey

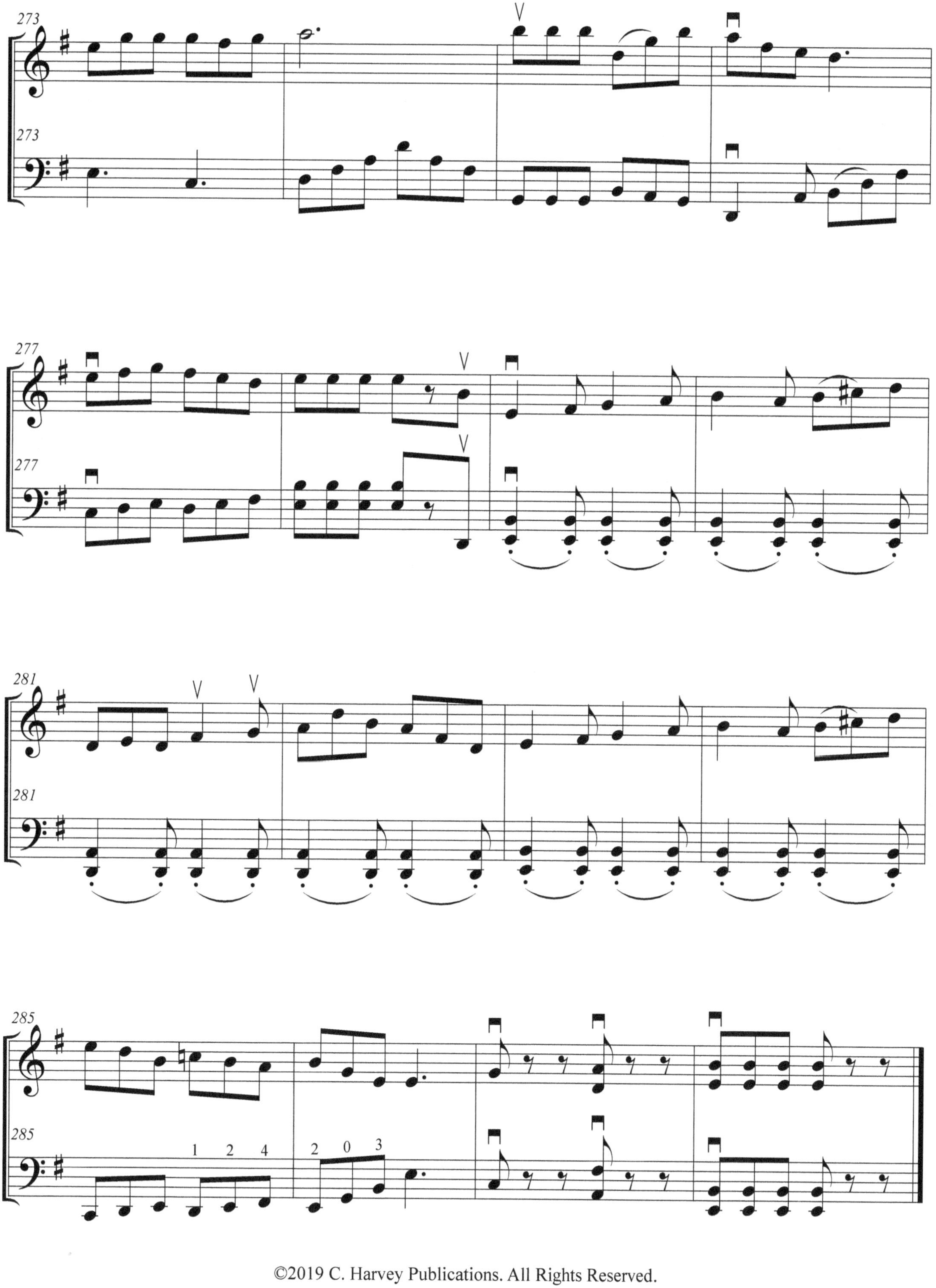

1812 Quickstep

Trad., arr. M. Harvey

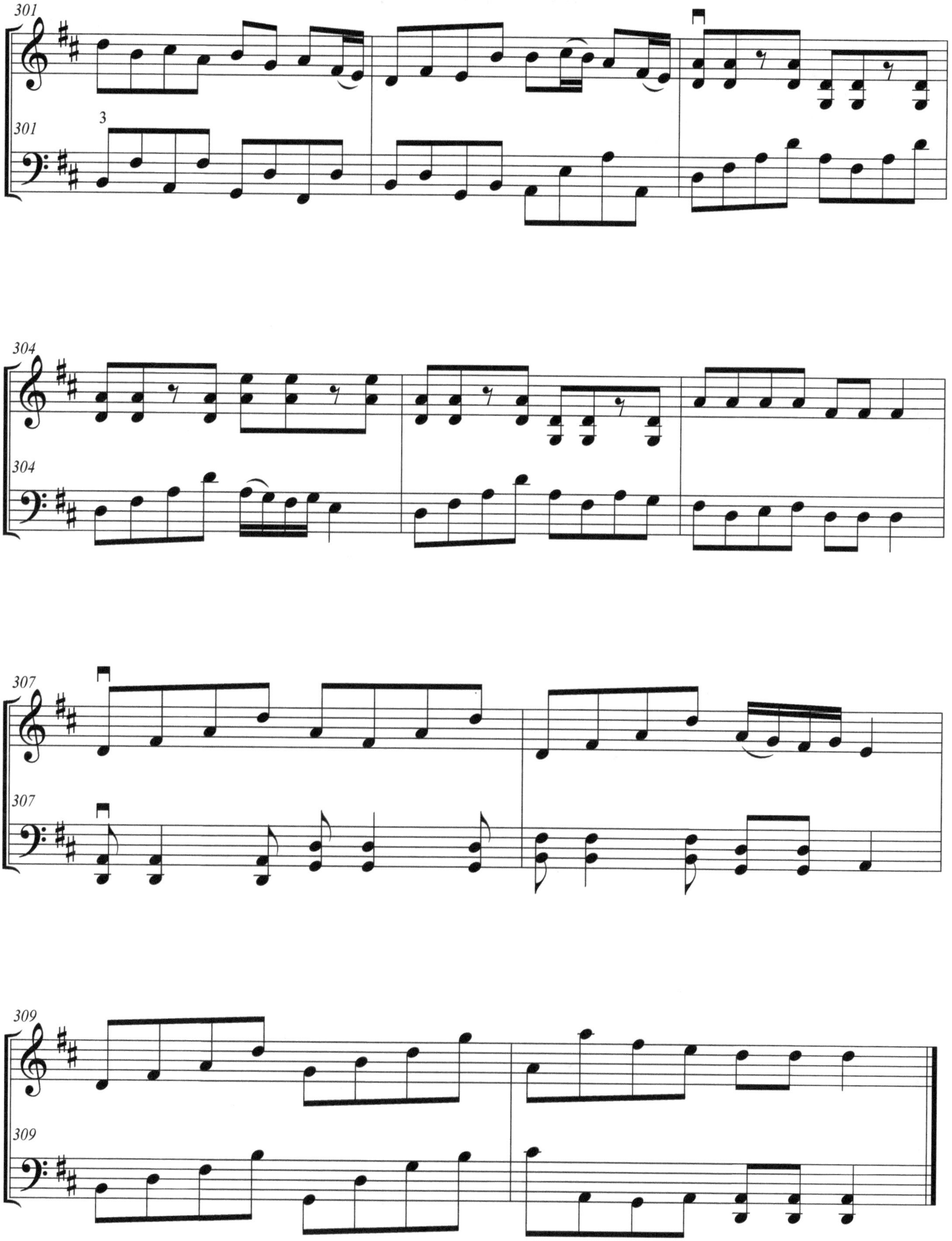

Shenandoah

Trad., arr. M. Harvey

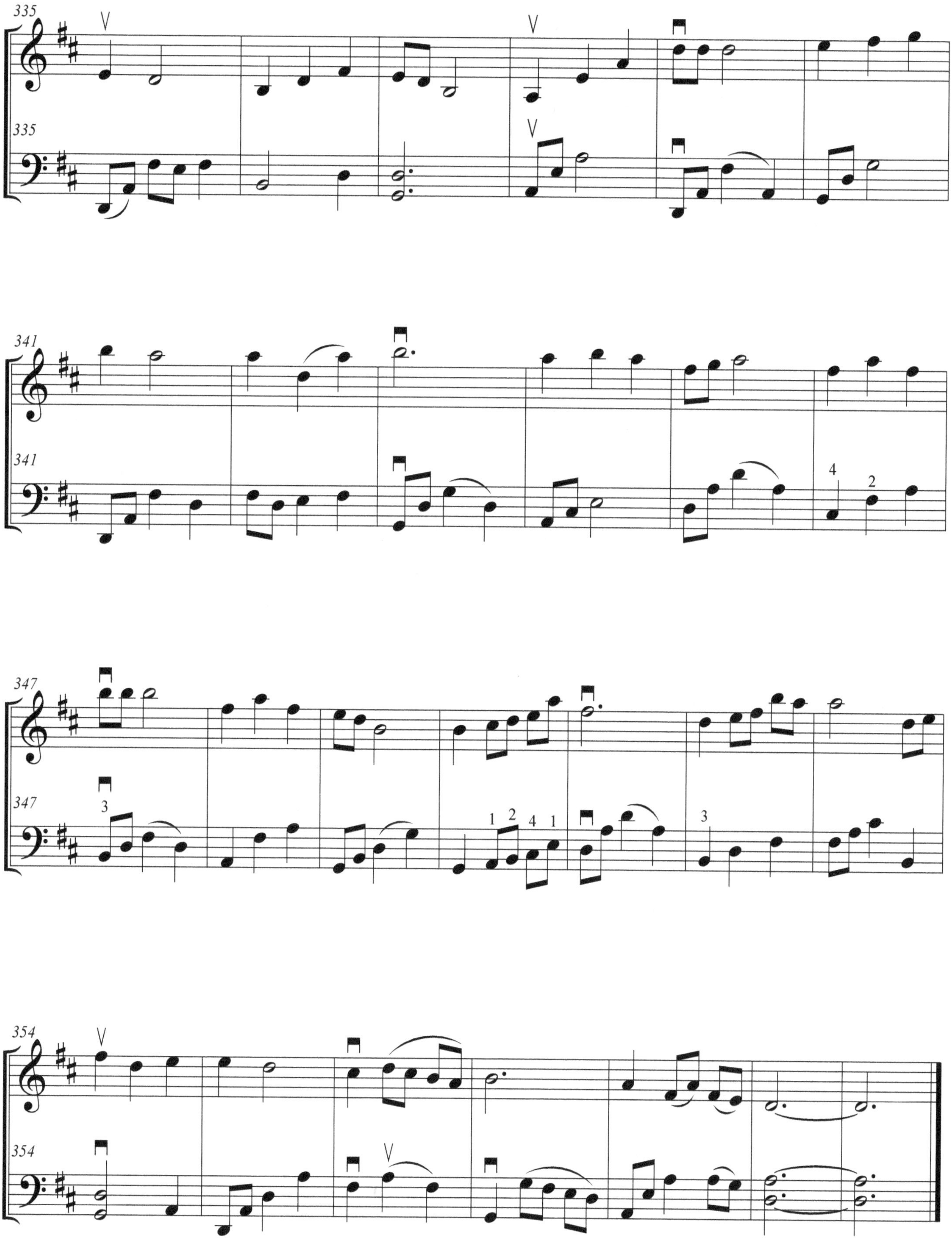
335
335
341
341
347
347
354
354

All the Pretty Horses

Trad., arr. M. Harvey

This Page Left Blank
to Eliminate Page Turns

Fire in the Mountain

Trad., arr. M. Harvey

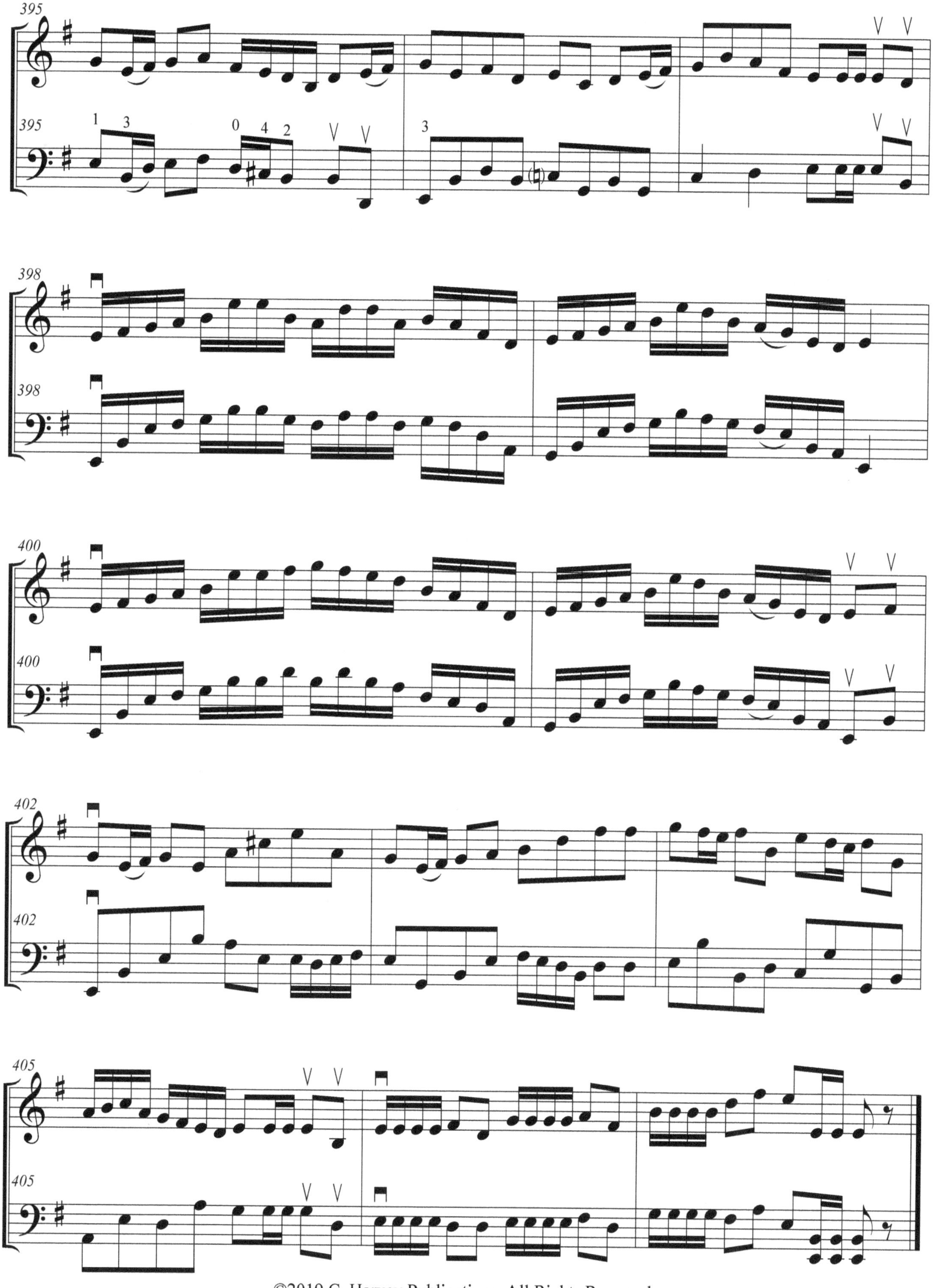
395
395
1 3
0 4 2
3
398
398
400
400
402
402
405
405

Devil Among the Tailors

Trad., arr. M. Harvey

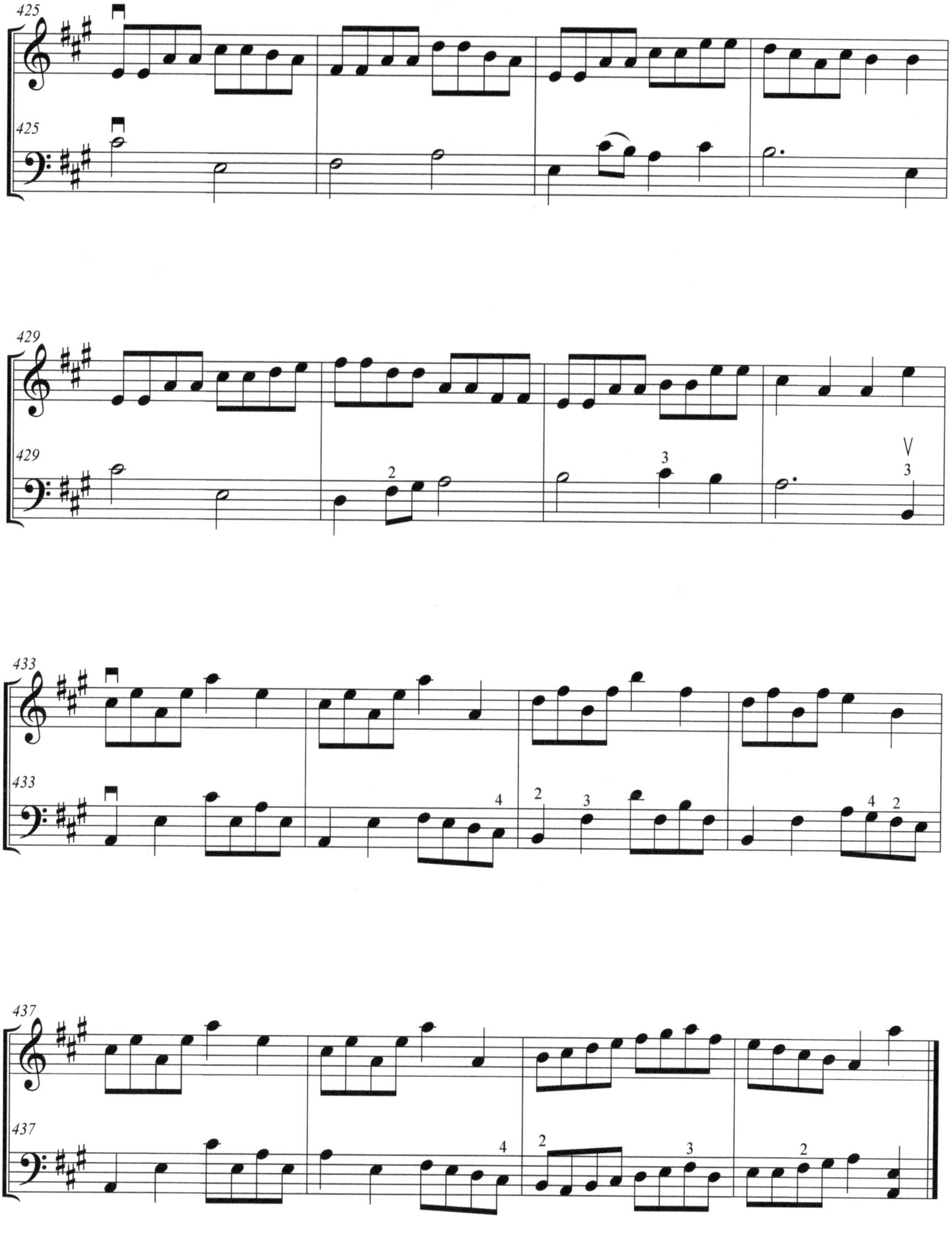
425
429
433
437

Liberty

Trad., arr. M. Harvey

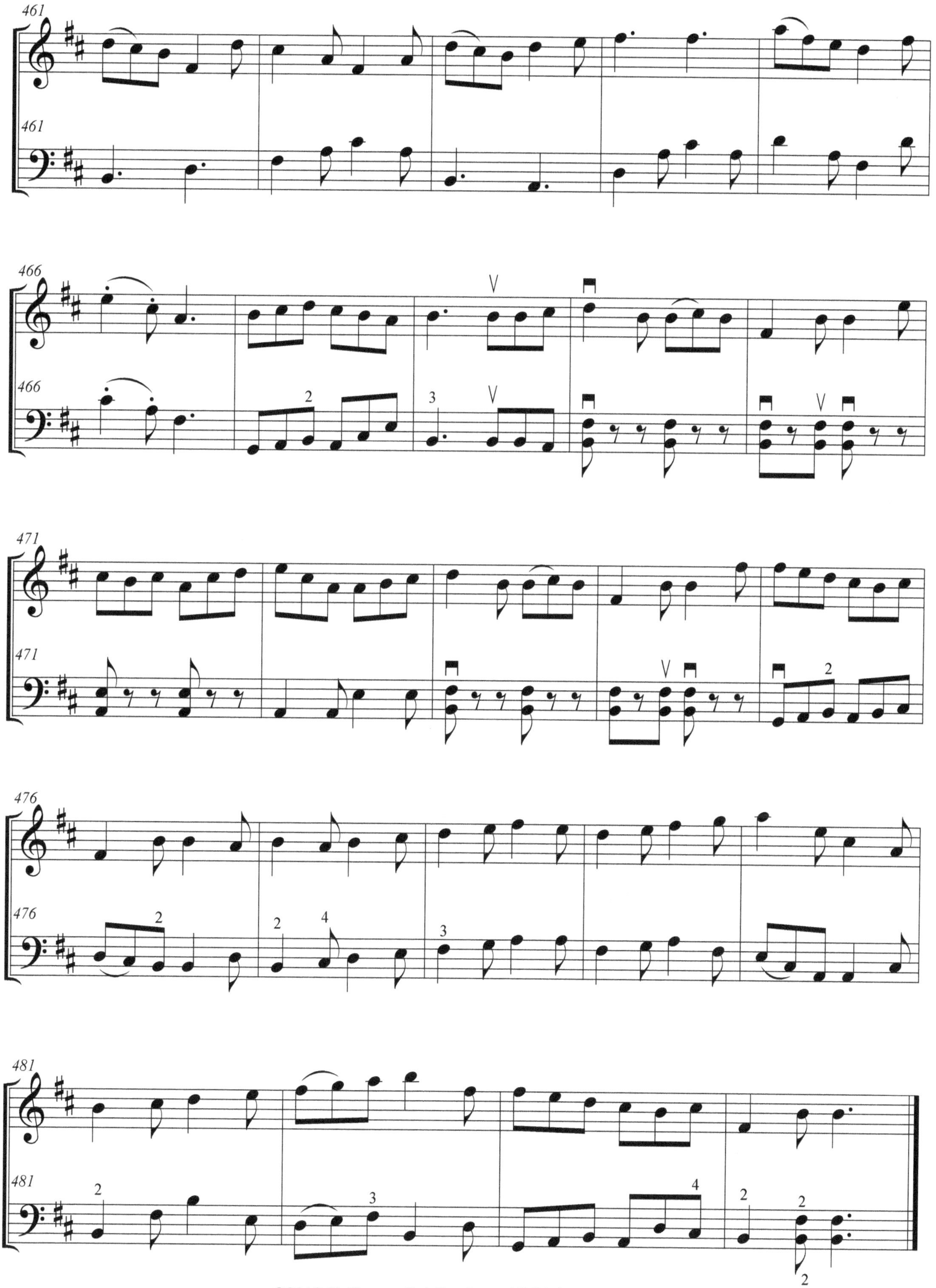

The Girl I Left Behind Me

Trad., arr. M. Harvey

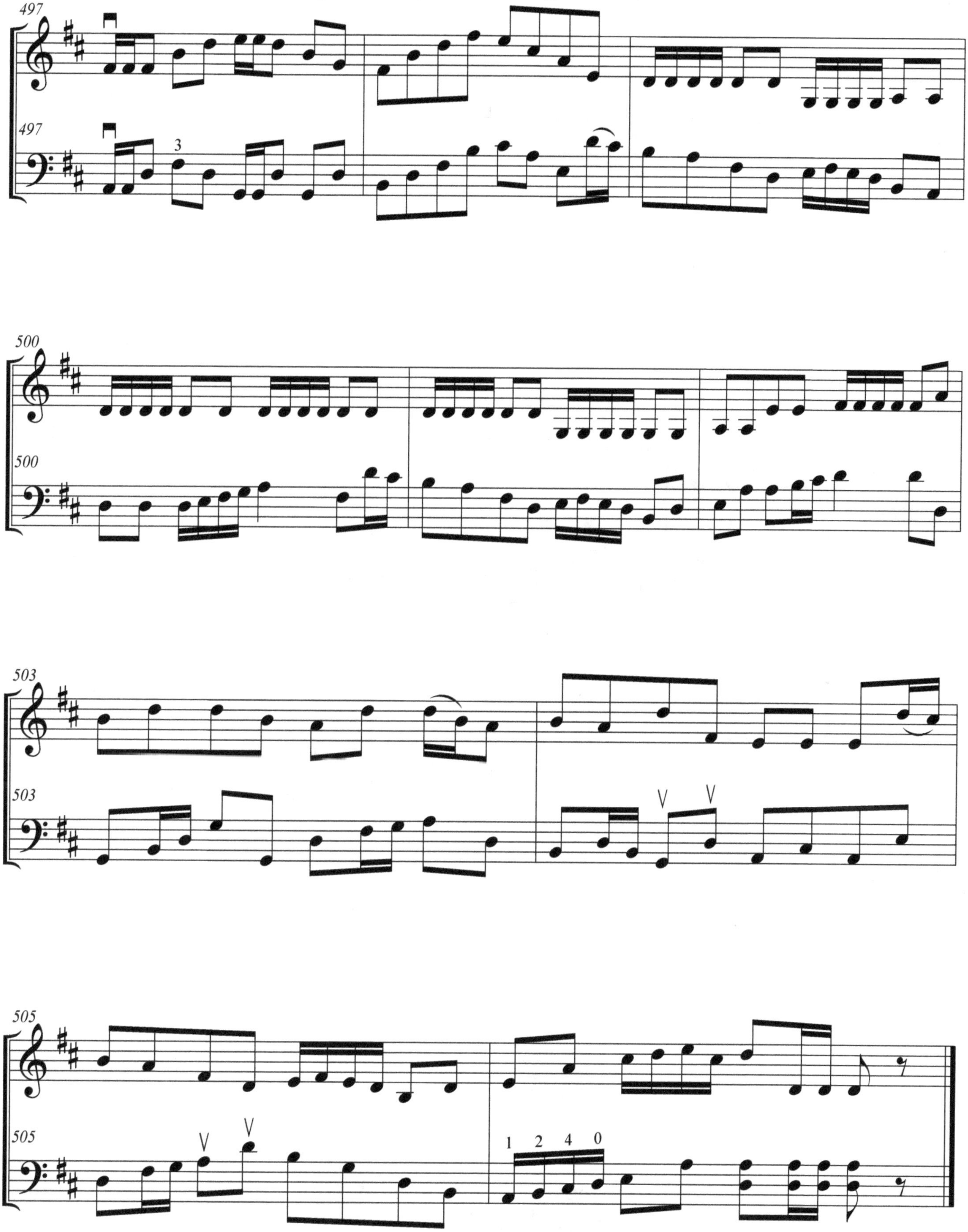
497
497
3
500
500
503
503
505
505
1 2 4 0

Ballad of the Green Mountain Boys

Trad., arr. M. Harvey

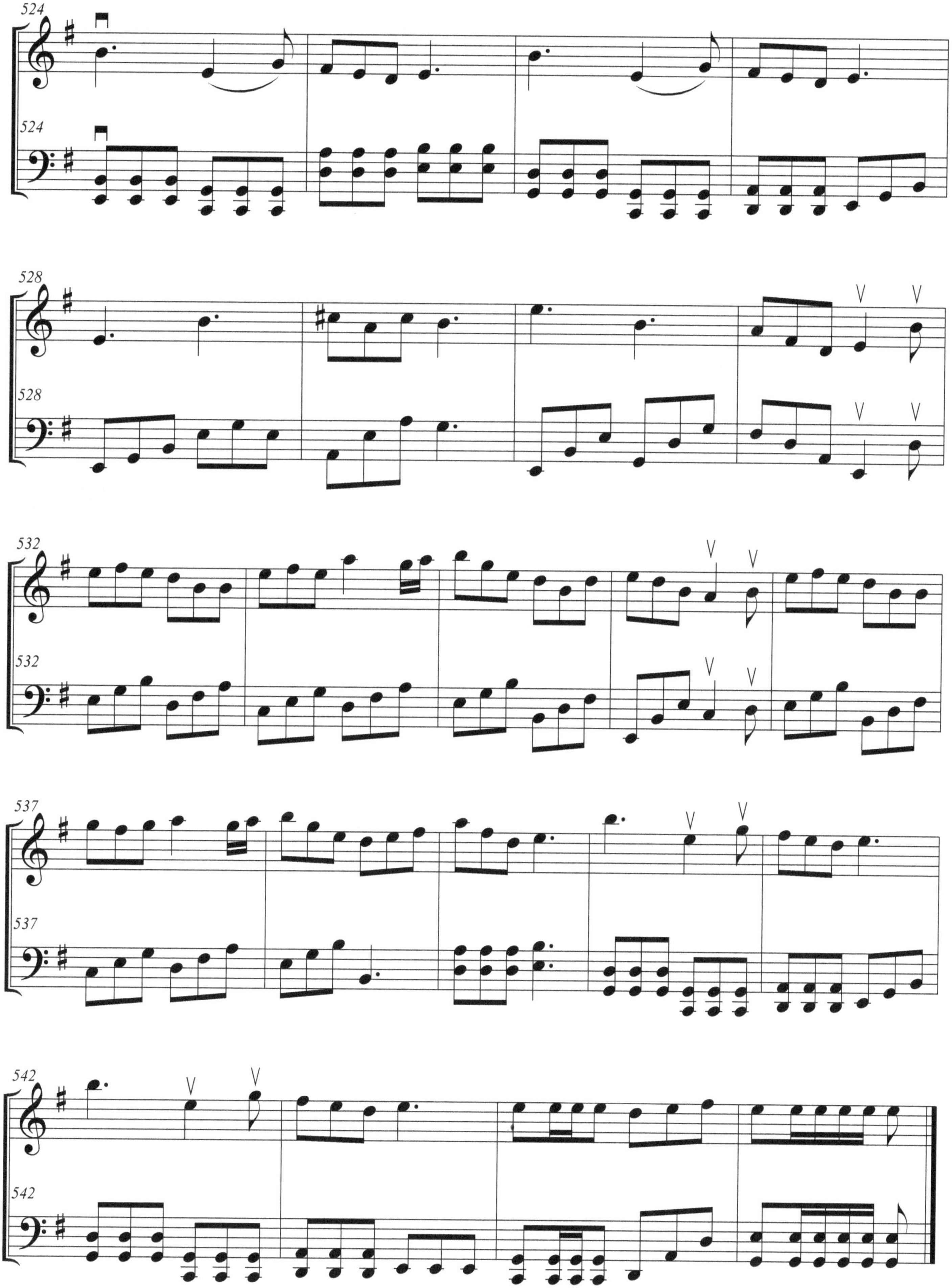
524
524
528
528
532
532
537
537
542
542

St. Patrick's Day

Trad., arr. M. Harvey

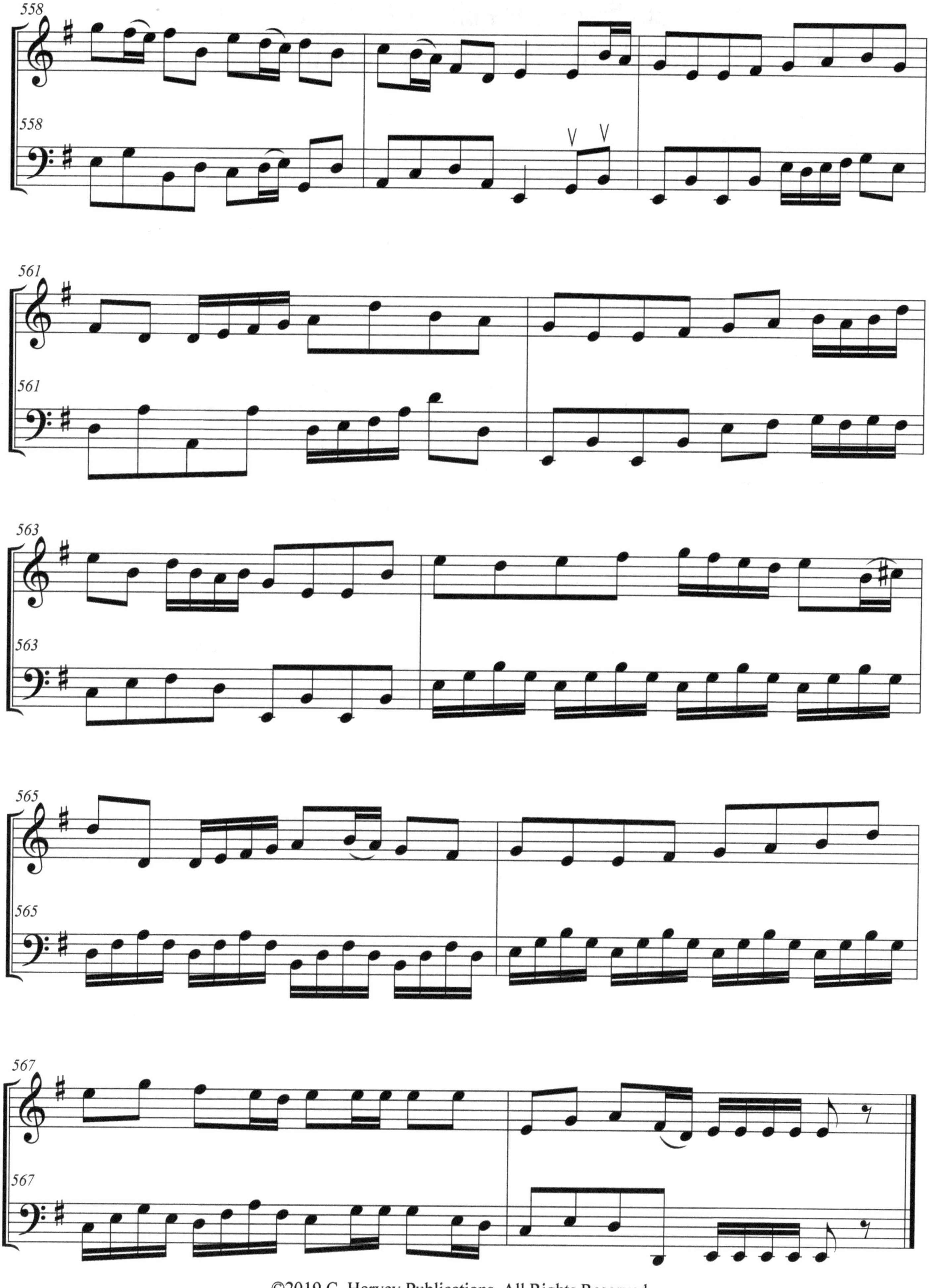
558
558
561
561
563
563
565
565
567
567

SAILING INTO BETHLEHEM

CHRISTMAS DUETS FOR TWO VIOLINS

all duets arranged by Myanna Harvey

Table of Contents

Sailing Into Bethlehem — Christmas Duets for Two Violins — We Wish You a Merry Christmas! — Traditional, arr. M. Harvey

CHP333

Sailing Into Bethlehem — Christmas Duets for Two Cellos — We Wish You a Merry Christmas! — Traditional, arr. M. Harvey

CHP334

Sailing Into Bethlehem — Christmas Duets for Two Violas — We Wish You a Merry Christmas! — Traditional, arr. M. Harvey

CHP335